Welcome to
LifeSearch!

If you urgently need to prepare to lead a LifeSearch group, turn the page and read QuickLead. QuickLead will give you enough information to get started.

LifeSearch hopes to help you and other persons within a small group explore topics about which you are concerned in your everyday living. We've tried to make LifeSearch

✔ immediately helpful to you;

✔ filled with practical ideas;

✔ Christian-oriented and biblically based;

✔ group building, so you will find companions in your mutual struggles and learning;

✔ easy for anyone to lead.

You have probably chosen to join with others in studying this Life-Search book because you feel some need. You may feel that need in your life strongly. Our hope for you is that by the time you complete the six chapters in this book with your LifeSearch group, you will have

✔ a better handle on how to meet the need you feel;

✔ some greater insights into yourself;

✔ a deeper understanding of how Christian faith can help you meet that need;

✔ a more profound relationship with God;

✔ new and/or richer relationships with the other persons in your LifeSearch group.

If you discover nothing else as part of this LifeSearch experience, we want you to learn this fact: *that you are not alone as you face life*. Other people have faced and still face the same problems, struggles, demands, and needs that you face. Some have advice to offer. Some have learned things the hard way—things they can now tell you about. Some can help you think through and talk through old concerns and new insights. Some can listen as you share what you've tried and what you want to achieve. Some even need what you can offer.

And you will never be alone because God stands with you.

The secret to LifeSearch is in the workings of your group. No two LifeSearch groups will ever be alike. Your LifeSearch group is made up of unique individuals—including you. All of you have much to offer one another. This LifeSearch book simply provides a framework for you and your group to work together in learning about an area of mutual concern.

We would like to hear what you think about LifeSearch and ways you can suggest for improving future LifeSearch books. A Mail-In Feedback survey appears in the back. Whether you lead the group or participate in it, please take the time to fill out the survey and mail it in to us.

IF YOU ARE LEADING A LifeSearch GROUP, please read the articles in the back of this book. These LifeSearch group leadership articles may answer the questions you have about leading your group.

IF YOU ARE PARTICIPATING IN A LifeSearch GROUP, BUT NOT LEADING IT, please read at least the article, "If You're Not Leading the Group." In any case, **you will benefit most if you come to your group meeting having read the chapter ahead of time and having attempted any assignments given in the previous chapter's "Before Next Time" sections.**

We want to remain helpful to you throughout your LifeSearch group experience. If you have any questions about using this LifeSearch book, please feel free to call Curric-U-Phone at 1-800-251-8591, and ask for the LifeSearch editor.

QUICKLEAD™

Look here for **QUICK** information about how to **LEAD** a session of LifeSearch. On LifeSearch pages, look for the following:

ICONS
Seven kinds of icons suggest different kinds of activities for your group to do at different points during the session (see page 4 for more information about ICONS).

MAIN TEXT: the "meat" of the session. Hopefully everyone will have read the MAIN TEXT ahead of time; if not, be prepared to offer a brief summary of the MAIN TEXT in your own words.

MARGINAL NOTES give you activity instructions and additional discussion starters.

CHAPTER THREE

LOOK BEYOND: WHAT DOES THE WORLD NEED NOW?

WORSHIP

Begin by praying this prayer:

O God of all people and places, we thank you for the marvelous diversity that you have created and placed in this world. We praise you for loving the world so much that you sent your son to be the light of this world. Inspire us to allow your loving light to shine in us and through us that the world might be transformed. In Christ's name, Amen.

CHECKING IN

Begin this session by welcoming any new persons to the group. Invite anyone to share significant events that may have occurred in their life since last time.

This time you will be looking beyond yourselves and the needs of persons in your congregation to the needs of persons in the world. Last time you were encouraged to visit a homeless shelter or community food pantry in your community or area. Or you may have visited a jail or talked with someone who works with the poor. These visits were intended to open your eyes to the needs of people in your area as you begin to reflect on how God wants to use your gifts for the transformation of the world into a community of justice and love.

DISCUSSION POINT

Debrief the members of the group on their visits using these questions and/or other questions as appropriate.

Spend some time reflecting on your visit to a shelter or food pantry. How many people does the shelter or pantry serve each month? Where do they get their resources? Where do they get their volunteers? Did you meet any of the clients of the shelter or pantry? How did you feel about being in such a setting? Does anyone in your group volunteer in ministries to the poor? What assistance does your church provide to the agencies that serve the poor? Has your church considered providing food or lodging for the poor? How does your congregation respond to emergency needs in your community? Who ministers to the needs of persons in jail or prison in your community? Has anyone in your congregation or community been on a short-term work-camp in this country or abroad? Has your community or area experienced a natural disaster such as a flood, earthquake, or hurricane? How did the church respond in that crisis? Are there any missionaries in your congregation or community who might reflect with you on the broader needs of our world? Please use these questions as a way to focus your attention on the needs of people beyond your own congregation.

If the group identifies such a missionary and wishes to do so, invite him or her to an extra session of your group to help members reflect about the needs around them.

SPIRITUAL GIFTS

UNDERLINED TEXT identify discussion starters inside the MAIN TEXT.

For more information, read the **LEADERSHIP ARTICLES** in the back of this LifeSearch book.

ICONS

ICONS are picture/symbols that show you at a glance what you should do with different parts of the main text at different times in the LIFESEARCH sessions.

The seven kinds of icons are

 WORSHIP—A prayer, hymn, or other act of worship is suggested at this place in the MAIN TEXT.

 CHECKING IN—At the beginning of each session, LIFESEARCH group members will be asked to "check in" with each other about what is happening in their lives. Sometimes group members will also be asked to "check in" about how their LIFESEARCH group experience seems to them.

 DISCUSSION POINT—Either the MAIN TEXT or a MARGINAL NOTE will suggest discussion starters. You will probably find more DISCUSSION POINTS than you can use in the usual LIFESEARCH session.

 GROUP INTERACTION—Either the MAIN TEXT or a MARGINAL NOTE will suggest a group activity that goes beyond a simple discussion within the whole group.

 BIBLE STUDY—At least once each session, your LIFESEARCH group will study a Bible passage together. Usually, DISCUSSION POINTS and/or GROUP INTERACTIONS are part of the BIBLE STUDY.

 WRITTEN REFLECTION—The MAIN TEXT will contain one or more suggestions for individuals to reflect personally on an issue. Space will be provided within the MAIN TEXT for writing down reflections. Sometimes individuals will be invited to share their written reflections if they wish.

 BEFORE NEXT TIME—In most sessions, your LIFESEARCH group members will be asked to do something on their own before the next time you meet together.

INTRODUCTION

"Hey mister. Why are you murdering that tree? You should take care of the Earth."

The saw was still in my hand. I had been caught in the act! I was cutting down a small shrub that had died during the previous winter. While I prepared the shrub for the chipping service so that it could be added to the city compost pile, several neighborhood children confronted me with similar words of condemnation. Despite my great sense of guilt and community humiliation, I was impressed with the strength of conviction and the expression of environmental concern that was shared by the children who were so willing to confront an adult with such a serious crime.

During the past twenty years, environmental education has been increasingly incorporated into schools and into the popular press. Most polls indicate that a high percentage of our population is committed to environmental protection issues. In spite of increased awareness and commitment to environmental issues that affect us directly, however, one senses a growing apathy concerning environmental problems that affect others and those that are global in nature. We do not want to allow environmental problems in our own back yards, but the same problems seem less important when they occur elsewhere, especially when they take place in areas where people have little power.

Environmental issues are often relegated to a secondary status because they are considered an unnecessary burden that obstructs progress. Although many new jobs have been created through the environmental movement, some see the movement as a threat to employment.

As stewards of God's creation, however, we have a responsibility to care for God's natural environment. It provides the resources we need for our survival and ensures the well-being of all future generations.

Most of us are deluged with information. During this age of information and communication, elections and efforts to develop social policy are sometimes determined by those who control the news media sound bites of the day. Complex issues that require long-term commitment are abandoned as "old news" if they are not solved before the next issue surfaces. We find it difficult to focus our attention when we need to juggle such issues as school reform, health-care concerns, parenting skills, racism, drugs, crime, national security and economic stagnation. We establish priorities and filter out the information that enables us to deal with those priorities. Apathy develops when we decide we lack the power to effect change in the areas we care about the most.

Following a session on "Hot Topics in Science" at the 1993 annual conference of the Association of Science-Technology Centers (ASTC), the program presenter explained that he had not addressed environmental concerns because he considered them a "sleeper" of a hot topic. How could protection of the natural world, God's creation, be considered a "sleeper" of an issue?

The environmental movement has been described as having progressed in several waves, including efforts for preservation, conservation and environmental protection. If the speaker from the ASTC conference is correct and environmental issues should now be considered a "sleeper" of a hot topic, we may be nearing the end of the most recent wave.

It is time to become reawakened to environmental concerns. This resource seeks to help persons take a new look at the environment. It depends on your active participation and your willingness to share experience and visions for the future. This resource attempts to frame issues in ways that will challenge common perceptions of the environment. Hopefully, it will help us widen our vision and strengthen our commitment to our life-long role as stewards of God's creation.

—Larry Dunlap-Berg

Reverend Larry Dunlap-Berg is an elder in the Northern Illinois Annual Conference of The United Methodist Church. Currently he is serving as the Coordinator of Exhibit Interpretation for the Cumberland Science Museum in Nashville, Tennessee. He holds a B.A. in geology from Case Western Reserve University in Cleveland, Ohio and earned the Master of Divinity degree from Garrett Evangelical Theological Seminary. He has done additional graduate study in geography and environmental science at Northeastern Illinois University in Chicago. He is married and the father of two daughters, Megan and Kristen.

CHAPTER ONE

IN THE BEGINNING

When the group is ready to begin, open by reading aloud the passage from Genesis 1 printed in the main text. Pray for God's guidance as you study and seek to be better stewards of the earth.

CHECKING IN

The gathering time helps build community and encourages a climate for open and honest sharing. At this time each session, group members will get to know other members by sharing events of the past week or by sharing research that may have been done for a group topic.

If you have a chalkboard or newsprint available, write down the reasons why persons have joined this study group. Record this information so that you can come back to it at the end of the study to determine to what degree expectations have been met.

Beginning Your LIFESEARCH Group

"Then God said, 'Let us make humankind in our image, according to our likeness; and let them have dominion over the fish of the sea, and over the birds of the air, and over the cattle, and over all the wild animals of the earth, and over every creeping thing that creeps upon the earth.' "

"God blessed them, and God said to them, 'Be fruitful and multiply, and fill the earth and subdue it; and have dominion over the fish of the sea and over the birds of the air and over every living thing that moves upon the earth' " (Genesis 1:26,28).

For this first session, be prepared to share in turn (1) your name; (2) brief information about your family, work, and leisure activities; and (3) why you have chosen to be a part of this LIFESEARCH group.

Throughout history, people have made controversial decisions that have led to incredible discoveries. First efforts at space flight and organ-transplant surgery represent hundreds of major technological advances once viewed as controversial, but now accepted as normal.

Often decisions to pursue such efforts are criticized when they are initiated. The decision makers are accused of "playing God." When we make such decisions, are we fulfilling a mandate to "be fruitful . . . and fill the earth and subdue it"? Or should we limit the ways we use technology in the pursuit of improving God's creation?

In the movie *Jurassic Park,* the park's founder called creation a matter of human will. While it is unlikely that a real Jurassic Park will be created in the near future, recent scientific discoveries and technological developments pose new life options unthought of even a few years ago.

Another view of creation and the God-human-environment relationship is expressed in this quote from a speech delivered by Chief Seattle in 1854:

DISCUSSION POINT

When we make such decisions, are we fulfilling a mandate to "be fruitful . . . and fill the earth and subdue it"? Or should we limit the ways we use technology in the pursuit of improving God's creation?

"This we know: The earth does not belong to [us], we belong to the earth. This we know: All things are connected like the blood which unites one family. All things are connected. Whatever befalls the earth befalls the [children] of the earth. [We] did not weave the web of life; [we are] merely a strand in it. Whatever [we] do to the web, [we] do to [ourselves]" (*Pro-Earth*, page 3).

Our understanding of the environment can range from global concerns such as rainforest preservation or the greenhouse effect to personal concerns such as our health or economic condition.

In this session we will investigate how our view of creation influences our response to new options for our lives. We will also explore our understanding of our role as part of God's creation.

You Are an Environment!

GROUP INTERACTION

As your LIFESEARCH group leader reads the following words, close your eyes, and remain silent:

Natural Resources	Appropriate Technology
Pollution	Unemployment
Wilderness	Litter
Northern Spotted Owl	Smokestacks
Mountains	Government Regulation
Open Spaces	Rainforests
Future Generations	Good Health
Global Warming	Endangered Animals
Ozone	Hazardous Waste
Clean-up Activities	Relaxation
Natural Beauty	

WRITTEN REFLECTION

After everyone has completed this task, give each person an opportunity to share the sentences that she or he wrote.

On newsprint or separate piece of paper, write the feelings and images that come to mind when you think of the word *environment*.

Making the "Right" Choice

When our youngest daughter was six months old, she had heart surgery for tetrology of Fallot, a congenital heart defect whose victims are commonly referred to as "blue babies." While Kristen was in the operating room, our insurance agent notified my wife and me that the insurance company would not pay for the surgery. The insurer did not consider surgery to be "medically necessary," even though the cardiologist and surgeon had rushed Kristen into emergency surgery because they believed she would not survive without the operation.

Both the surgeon and the insurer were "playing God," but their solutions were contradictory. My wife and I had to choose between the following options for how we would entrust Kristen's care to those who chose to "play God":

1) We could play God ourselves by declining the suggested medical procedures because we denied the problem or viewed Kristen's condition as God's will.

2) We could entrust Kristen's future to a claims agent who was more concerned with the insurance company's financial condition than our daughter's medical need.

3) We could rely on a surgical team who claimed to have the skills and knowledge necessary to create a miraculous recovery from a desperate situation.

After Kristen's successful operation, one of my co-workers told me his brother had died from the same condition several years earlier because the medical procedures used for Kristen were not yet developed. Following subsequent open-heart surgery, our energetic kindergartner now is proud to show us her scar and to tell us the doctors gave it to her so she would always remember them and how they had taken care of her.

I am confident the surgical team used appropriate technologies and procedures, but these same techniques were not available to children in any previous generation, nor would they be available to many children who live in poverty. The use of many new technological advances raises serious ethical and theological concerns that must be explored carefully. <u>In our quest to use the earth's resources to create life-giving miracles, how should we decide which technologies and procedures are appropriate?</u>

According to Roy Martin, a medical ethicist and senior chaplain at Cook/Fort-Worth, Texas Children's Medical Center, "two things have collided in the history of Western Civilization. With the advance of science, we almost have this terrible compulsion that says, 'If we can do something, we must do it. If we have the technology to do it, we should.' That's not always the right choice."

A Dilemma of a Research Team

Imagine you are on a research team that is studying a group of children who have a genetic abnormality. Your team has made several intriguing discoveries.

DISCUSSION POINT

Which of these options would you choose? Why?

DISCUSSION POINT

How do you feel about using available technology to create life-giving miracles?

Should the technology always—or usually—be used?

What theological and ethical concerns need to be explored?

GROUP INTERACTION

Divide your LIFESEARCH group into smaller groups of three to five persons, if necessary. Instruct them to read through the dilemma and to follow the instructions given in the boldface print in the margin.

You are asked to make a recommendation concerning whether this new procedure should be made available. Include your reasons for support and opposition. If the technique will be used, propose methods of funding and decide for whom the technique should become available.

Your discussion of this topic should include any knowledge you have gained from similar situations. Also consider your knowledge of Scripture and the church's historical response to similar situations. Combine your knowledge, experience, and reasoning powers to develop the theological stance with which your group is most comfortable.

DISCUSSION POINT

Ask small groups to report on their work on the dilemma. Then as a larger group discuss the questions presented in the main text.

You are investigating whether members of the study group have a special ability to communicate with ocean mammals. This phenomenon was first reported by parents whose child showed a dramatic increase in verbal skills after a brief encounter with a whale. Preliminary indications are that some children in the study group have a mutually beneficial means of communication with whales that could help to unlock valuable information about marine life.

Some persons with this condition lead normal lives and have few difficulties. Many, however, require lifelong specialized medical and daycare provisions that create severe financial burdens for their families. Their life expectancy is much lower than average. Many persons with this condition are not accepted into mainstream society.

You are interviewing the families of the study group. Some families feel overwhelmed by their children's current and anticipated special needs. Most, however, demonstrate a special closeness and an ability to focus their efforts, overcome obstacles and face their lives with unique energy and enthusiasm. This inner strength helps many families gain new and positive life perspectives.

Recently your team discovered a technique for detecting and correcting this genetic abnormality before birth. Because this high-risk procedure, which has a fifty percent success rate, is extremely expensive, availability is limited to those who can afford it. An advocacy group proposed that adequate funding be secured so that the procedure might be made available to all persons. No one has proposed a method for raising such funds.

1) Does God's creation, including the human genetic code, provide infinite resources that we are free to manipulate and exploit for our own purposes?

2) Should genetic abnormalities be altered in the way that is being proposed in this scenario?

3) Did you feel as though you were "playing God" when you made your decisions? How did you feel?

Exploring the Language in Our Lease: What Is *Dominion*, Anyway?

Some wayward stranger in a spacecraft, coming from some other part of the heavens, could look at earth and never know

DISCUSSION POINT

Recall when you first saw a photograph of earth taken from space. What were your thoughts? feelings? reactions?

GROUP INTERACTION

In groups of three to five persons, define the word domin-ion. *Ask groups to compare the way you define the word to definitions found in a regular dictionary and in a Bible dictionary. Ask: How do these definitions compare with Hall's statement? (You will need to have one or more regular dictionaries and Bible dictionaries available.)*

DISCUSSION POINT

What does dominion over the earth mean? Are we called to be earth keepers or earth movers?

that it was inhabited at all. But that same wayward stranger would certainly know instinctively that if the earth were inhabited, then the destinies of all who lived on it must inevitably be interwoven and joined. We are one hunk of ground, water, air, clouds, floating around in space. From out there it really is "one World" (Frank Borman, Apollo 8, December 24, 1969).

Images and technologies from international efforts in space exploration revolutionized our view of the world. Reactions to photographs of the earth from space resulted in new ways of understanding humanity's place in God's creation. The concept of spaceship earth confirmed that the earth has limits, that we need to learn to live within those limits, and that we have a responsibility to care for the earth's limited resources. This perspective is similar to that stated nearly 150 years ago by Chief Seattle.

Another view is that nature is here for us to tame, use, sub-due, conquer, and dominate. "This has been the dominant attitude from the beginning of the Modern era into our own time. And we, today, are part of a society that has been built upon this premise. The idea that humanity is nature's 'lord and possessor,' capable of making over what God rather thoughtlessly put together in the first place, is an almost exact description of the North American attitude towards the natural universe. It is our very birthright" (Douglas John Hall, "Loving Creation," *Pro-Earth*, page 5).

Although advocates of both perspectives claim support from the Bible and from religious tradition, the church often has been blamed for human actions that have harmed the earth's environment. Critics of the Judeo-Christian tradition point to the creation stories in Genesis as the root cause of human efforts to dominate the earth. The problem seems to stem from our interpretation of the mandate that we should have domin-ion over the earth.

All Living Things Change Their Environment

All living things change their environment. They act together to create cycles in nature through which nutrients and energy flow. Often the waste byproduct of one living organism enables another organism's survival. For example, through photosynthesis, plants act as factories to use the sun's energy, carbon dioxide, water, and soil nutrients to produce their food. Oxygen, a waste product of this photosynthesis, is essential for the respiration of animals.

Whether they eat plants, or plant-eating animals, animals help to close the circles of energy and nutrient flow. A waste product of their respiration is the carbon dioxide necessary for photosynthesis. Microscopic organisms help to return nutrients to the soil by accelerating the decomposition processes of dead organisms.

Through digging, burrowing, nest building and other such activities, living organisms alter the physical characteristics of their surroundings.

DISCUSSION POINT

What examples of these statements can you identify?

At times, the activities of one type of organism clash with the basic needs of another organism. Throughout history, those clashes, along with changes in habitats caused by climate, geologic forces, and astronomical events, have led to the endangerment and extinction of various species.

One can find parallel activities in nature for most human activities that alter our environment. The major differences are the scope, intensity, and speed of those activities. Through the use of various technologies, we make intentional and unintentional changes in our local surroundings. Such changes can lead to dramatic and irreversible breaks in global cycles in nature, thereby affecting all current and future life.

BIBLE STUDY

Read the Creation stories recorded in Genesis 1 and 2. These chapters contain two distinct stories of the Creation of the world. In the first story (Genesis 1:1-2:4a), humans are created after plants and animals. In the second version (Genesis 2:4b-25), the first man is created prior to plants, animals, and the first woman. Regardless of the differences, clearly in each story God's creative hand is emphasized—and readers stand even today in wonder! God created order from chaos—nothingness.

These two Creation stories, although different, portray God as a purposeful, gracious God, whose creation reflects grace and design. Today we, like ancient people before us, ponder such questions as: Why am I here? What is my role in the created order?

"What are human beings that you are mindful of them, mortals that you care for them? (Psalm 8:4)

A recent hymn provides this answer:

O God who shaped creation at earth's chaotic dawn,
your word of power was spoken, and lo! the dark was gone!
You framed us in your image, you brought us into birth,
you blessed our infant footsteps and shared your splendored
earth.

O God, with pain and anguish a mother sees her child
embark on dead-end pathways, alluring, but defiled;
so too your heart is broken when hate and lust increase,
when worlds you birthed and nurtured spurn ways that lead to
peace.

(From "O God Who Shaped Creation," *The United Methodist Hymnal*, No. 443; Copyright © 1989 The
United Methodist Publishing House.)

DISCUSSION POINT

After taking a few minutes to reflect on the questions in the main text, move into a discussion of humanity's rights and responsibilities related to God's Creation.

WORSHIP

1) How does creation continue today? Describe your understanding of our role in God's creative process.

2) Are there limits to the types and the amount of tinkering we should do to God's creation?

3) How do you understand humanity's responsibility to subdue the earth and to have dominion over every living thing?

As you end this session, record prayer concerns of group members in the space below.

Pray:
My God, you saw me in my unformed substance and numbered my days before I had lived one of them. Be close to me now, my God, help me to love you without restraint and to manage all the affairs of my life to the end that when I stand to give account, I need not be ashamed. In the name of my Lord, I pray. Amen.

CHAPTER TWO

MANY GIFTS, ONE SPIRIT

WORSHIP

When the group is ready to begin, open with this prayer or one in your own words.

CHECKING IN

If there are new persons in the group today, take a few moments to allow them to introduce themselves, and invite other group members to tell who they are. Invite persons to share a fresh insight stemming from the last session. This would also be an appropriate time for persons to share any joys or concerns.

Begin by praying this prayer:

Our God, we praise you for the wonders of your creation. It is very good! May we proclaim our gratitude for the beauty of nature and the blessings of humankind! Help us to look at those around us with eyes of joy and compassion; in Christ's name. Amen.

Read aloud Genesis 1:11-25.

According to Genesis 1, God stated repeatedly that Creation was good. Upon completion of Creation, God saw everything, . . .and indeed it was very good. Throughout history, Christians have sung praise and proclaimed gratitude for the Earth's beauty.

In this session we will explore our understanding of the wonder, magnitude, and complexity of life on Earth.

Spine-Tingling Images!

I once served as pastor of an inner-city church in a community with a severe shortage of adequate housing for low-income residents. I was saddened when the city demolished several large apartment buildings to clear space for a new police station. The day after the demolition was completed, however, I experienced a tremendous feeling of liberation while walking past the corner that had become a focal point for nearly ten years of work as a church and community worker, seminary student, and pastor.

The space that had been occupied by bricks, glass, and human activity was now an open area filled with sunlight, "fresh city air," and even a few birds and squirrels. It helped me to reflect on the importance of open spaces in our lives. While modern society tends to simplify our environment in the name of increased efficiency and production, encounters with nature renew the human spirit. This encounter helped me to reflect on several images of significance to me:

—As a preschooler, I spent much of my time lying on my back under a large, white sycamore tree. I felt tiny, yet peaceful, and part of something larger as I watched the tree's branches sway in the breeze as clouds passed by.

—As an elementary school student, I accompanied my father to streams, ponds, and forests to collect water creatures and insects for use in his high school biology classes.

—As a college student on a geology field trip to Death Valley, I awakened each morning, surrounded by mountains, clear skies, petrified wood, rope lava, desert vegetation such as cacti and yucca plants, or incredible geologic formations.

—As a science teacher and church volunteer in Puerto Rico, I watched excited students as we went on field trips to see the tremendous variations in plant and animal life at the beaches, in the rainforest, in the mountains, on the mangrove islands, and in near-desert conditions.

WRITTEN REFLECTION

Ask persons individually to follow the instructions in the main text. After all have completed this task, give participants an opportunity to share their reflections on the goodness of creation.

Silently reflect on your spine-tingling encounters with the natural world: those times you would agree with the proclamation that "Indeed, it was very good." In the space provided below, share the feelings and images that come to mind.

BIBLE STUDY

Read again Genesis 1:11-25.

The Hebrews believed that the universe was not created by chance. Rather Creation was the purposeful design of a gracious, loving God.

DISCUSSION POINT

What questions have you heard younger children ask when they hear the Creation stories?

How have you answered those questions?

Genesis 1:11-13 reminds us of the goodness of the earth, from which grain springs to feed those who roam the earth, and out of which minerals can be dug to meet the increasing demands of a growing civilization.

The waters of the world (verses 20-23) are embued with beauty and riches—treasures of fish to feed and delight populations.

Birds (verses 21-23) and animals (verses 24-31), from the small to the large, likewise enrich the earth.

GROUP INTERACTION

Ask group members to describe to a partner an event in their lives in which they strongly felt the wonder of Creation.

Sit with a small child in the woods, by a mountain stream, in the midst of a city park, or in some other relatively untouched, natural setting. Often the question comes, How did this all come to be? Once again, as we struggle to answer the child, we are struck by the wonder of it all!

God Created It. . .We Perfected It?

We find it hard to think of the earth as being vulnerable. Surely extinctions have been occurring for millions of years, yet hasn't nature always proved resilient? While in ages past one animal or plant species became extinct every one hundred and ninty or so years, today it is one every twenty minutes. If every threatened species is a flashing warning light, then the whole world must be ablaze with the lights of impending plant and animal extinctions (*Save the Birds*, page 22).

A recent magazine advertisement proclaimed that "God created it. . . Bijan refined it!" The advertisement referred to "DNA"—a new fragrance for men. The product was packaged in a double helix-shaped bottle. Through this clever slogan, the creators of this marketing ploy provided a simple description of thousands of years of effort by the human species to "perfect" God's creation for *our* short-term benefit.

For about one hundred and fifty years, scientists have used a system developed by Carolus Linnaeus to classify all living species of plants and animals. As of today, fewer than two million species of plants and animals are classified, but scientists have predicted that the total number ranges between five million and eight million species. One of the main reasons for this wide discrepancy is the huge number of insects found recently as part of rainforest research. Many species will become extinct before they are discovered and classified.

Despite this huge gap in knowledge, scientists have discovered invaluable clues to how the natural world works. Ecosystems are communities of plants, animals, and non-living materials that interact with one another. Soil provides nutrients, and plants produce food. Animals consume plants or other animals, and bacteria and fungi decompose dead plants and animals to return nutrients to the soil. Each part of an ecosystem has a specific job.

Exploding Growth of Population

Our planet developed its diversity over billions of years. The resulting genetic pool enables plant and animal life to adapt to environmental changes. The richness of this genetic pool provides life with insurance for the future. It serves as the source for new medicines, foods, and products, and offers the potential for future adaptations.

Natural communities of plants and animals are usually complex and diverse, with mixed populations. Modern methods of development, however, often replace diverse communities with single-species crops. These monocultures are popularly viewed as an improvement because their products improve properties such as strength, taste, or the ease of harvesting and processing for market use.

Through these "advancements," however, wild populations are reduced in number and range. Because of a lack of diversity, the species that replace them are often highly susceptible to diseases or pests.

Until about ten thousand years ago, the Earth's capacity to support the human species limited the number of people on Earth to a few million. Because of human efforts to grow crops and keep livestock, this number increased to about 350 million persons by the early 1500's.

This explosion in the human population was accompanied by localized losses of natural habitats. Many plant and animal species were sacrificed for this expansion of human life. Some species suffered the reduction of habitat, others became extinct.

Because of human efforts to control the environment and to spread into Australia, North America, and South America, the Earth's carrying capacity for humans continued to increase. By the nineteenth century, the world's human population had increased to more than 900 million. During this time, these areas lost many of their natural habitats.

Human population reached about 1.6 billion by the beginning of the twentieth century. This growth was fueled by new technologies which evolved due to the ability to mine and use fossil fuels. These energy sources took millions of years to develop from the buried remains of ancient plants and animals. Today the known reserves of these fuels are dwindling at an alarming rate because they are being consumed so quickly. Many large untouched, unexplored, and undeveloped areas remained at the beginning of this century.

Environmental changes were limited to localized areas until people developed the ability to use air transportation and mass communications to bring all people on Earth into closer contact with one another. By 1950, the number of humans

World Population Growth

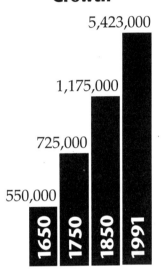

5,423,000

1,175,000

725,000

550,000

1650 1750 1850 1991

totaled 2.5 billion. This growth, accompanied by an increased per-capita consumption of natural resources, resulted in increased air and water pollution. Widespread concern developed about the cumulative effects on living species of exposure to radiation, pesticides, and the impact of municipal and industrial toxic wastes.

By 1993 the world's population more than doubled again to 5.4 billion people. Today local problems with environmental degradation are often overshadowed by global concerns. The Earth's capacity to care for other species is being eroded, and species of plants and animals are being extinguished rapidly. Natural habitats in the air, water, soil, and forest are being destroyed by agricultural and industrial encroachment and the rapid consumption of natural resources and production of wastes. These pressures increase rapidly as the population and economic activity of humans continue their explosive growth.

An additional environmental problem is that many third-world countries desperately need the benefits of industrialized economic development. This eco-justice issue creates a dilemma that begs for careful resolution. While the quality of life must be improved in these areas, the Earth's delicate ecological balance cannot afford to repeat the trauma it endured during previous industrial development.

(1) It has been estimated that the rate of plant and animal extinctions has increased from one each 190 years to one each twenty minutes. This has been linked to the rapid expansion of the human population. <u>Do you accept this analysis? If so, is this situation acceptable? If not, how could this situation be corrected?</u>

(2) <u>How do you determine the value of a species? Do you determine it by its economic value in the marketplace? by its potential as a future source of food, medicine, or other products? by its value as a unique part of God's creation? Should all species be protected at any cost, or are some species more expendable than others? If some are more valuable than others, how do you determine their value?</u>

(3) Many third-world countries hope to acquire technologies that provide significant short-term economic benefits, which have led to serious environmental problems in other places. <u>Should these technologies be used regardless of the environmental consequences, or should these countries be limited to the use of Earth-friendly technologies? Who should have the right to make a decision to limit such technologies because</u>

DISCUSSION POINT

After reflecting on the preceding information, ask groups of three to five persons to discuss the questions in the main text.

of environmental risk? Is it possible to have economic development that provides jobs and improves environmental quality?

Jobs Versus Species Preservation

Imagine you live in a community that has the last known spawning area for a fish that has been classified as endangered. For several years a resource management team has worked to save and to improve the environmental quality.

These efforts are applauded by environmental groups from around the world. From the beginning, each step of your community's habitat-restoration effort has been documented as part of a long-term university research project.

The future of this project is threatened by a recent event in your community. An entertainment company that is the second largest employer in the area announces expansion plans that will destroy the spawning area. They argue that this facility will produce many jobs. Furthermore, the company is asking the local government to support this expansion through tax incentives and government insured low-interest loans.

Your community is split evenly between the two sides in this dispute. Company representatives contend that a hearing is not needed because the fish has no commercial value. Project supporters produce a bumper sticker that reads, "Eat Fish, Save Jobs!"

Those who oppose the project maintain that any loss of jobs will be minimal compared to those which will result from internal management decisions of the entertainment company. These jobs will be lost due to increases in efficiency as the company reorganizes its staffing configuration and becomes more automated. A local newspaper has obtained a copy of a company memo marked "Confidential" that supports this contention. Company officials have confirmed the existence of the memo, but they contend that its contents are being taken out of context. All parties accept that there will be numerous court battles before this matter is resolved.

By holding a hearing, your local government is attempting to collect information that will be evaluated before a final decision is made on whether or not to support this expansion project.

This hearing will include representatives from (1) the habitat-restoration effort, (2) the entertainment company proposing the project, and (3) the local government.

GROUP INTERACTION

Read through the case study.

Form three equal groups to represent the participants in this hearing. The remaining members of your group will assume the roles of hearing officers.

Instructions for the hearing officers: (1) Allow representatives from each side to take turns while making presentations in support of their point of view. (2) Ask questions at the conclusion of each presentation. (3) After all presentations have been made, vote on whether or not to support this project. As hearing officers announce their vote, be sure they explain their reasons for support or opposition.

Your discussion should include knowledge you have gained from similar situations. Also include your knowledge of Scripture and church tradition as part of your discussion. Consider the questions raised earlier. Be prepared to share how you felt during the roleplay.

BEFORE NEXT TIME

WORSHIP

In the next session you will explore how you view the relationship between God and humanity during times of natural disaster. In preparation for that session, be aware of the natural disasters that are a part of your time. Clip out and bring newspaper accounts of natural disasters. How do television or radio reporters report on storms, earthquakes, and other natural disasters? Come prepared to share your findings with others in the LIFESEARCH group next time.

Record in the space below any prayer concerns shared by members of your group:

Close by singing or reading the words to this hymn:

I Sing the Almighty Power of God

I sing the almighty power of God, that made the mountains rise,
that spread the flowing seas abroad, and built the lofty skies.
I sing the wisdom that ordained the sun to rule the day;
the moon shines full at God's command, and all the stars obey.

I sing the goodness of the Lord, who filled the earth with food,
who formed the creatures thru the Word, and then pronounced them
good.
Lord, how thy wonders are displayed, where'er I turn my eye,
if I survey the ground I tread, or gaze upon the sky.

There's not a plant or flower below, but makes thy glories known,
and clouds arise, and tempests blow, by order from thy throne;
while all that borrows life from thee is ever in thy care;
and everywhere that we can be, thou, God art present there.
(Isaac Watts, 1715)

Chapter Three

DON'T BURY YOUR TALENTS

WORSHIP

Begin this session by asking your group to read this greeting responsively.

CHECKING IN

Before starting on the discussion materials in this chapter, invite members of the group to share highlights in their lives since your group last met.

BIBLE STUDY

This we know, the earth does not belong to us.

We belong to the earth.

This we know, all things are connected.

Like the blood which unites one family, all things are connected.

Our God is the same God, whose compassion is equal for all.

For we did not weave the web of life.

We are merely a strand in it.

Whatever we do to the web we do to ourselves.

Let us give thanks for the web and the circle that connects us.

Thanks be to God, the God of all.

"Then the one who had received the one talent also came forward, saying, 'Master, . . .I went and hid your talent in the ground. Here you have what is yours.' But his master replied, 'You wicked and lazy slave! . . . you ought to have invested my money with the bankers, and on my return I would have received what was my own with interest'" (Matthew 25:24-27).

Read Matthew 25:14-30. After gaining a sense of the parable from a first reading, read the same passage a second time. This time, however, imagine yourself not as one of the human characters, but as one of the talents. (You need to know that a talent is a sizable sum of money, equal to more than the average laborer would have earned in fifteen years!) Imagine yourself as one of the talents that was invested, and as the one talent that was hid in a hole in the ground.

DISCUSSION POINT

Divide the larger group into smaller groups of three or four persons. Ask smaller groups to discuss the question: What insights did you gain when you imagined yourself as one of the talents?

What connections might you draw between this Bible passage and the problem of what you do with your material things once they outlive their normal usefulness?

Nearly eighty percent of the material that is buried in landfills could be recycled. These resources could be used again, but they are mixed up and deposited where they are no longer useful. In the parable of the talents, the servant who buried the talent was called wicked and lazy even though the talent had been retrieved. <u>What might the outcome have been had the master encountered a servant who had buried the talents but had not been able to retrieve them?</u>

In this session, we will explore our views on several issues related to responsible use of recyclable materials.

In Search of a Place Called "Away!"

"...desirable things happen to garbage mainly when someone stands to earn money by making desirable things happen. Good intentions alone don't count for much. Despite what people profess in opinion polls as to what they would 'be willing' to do with their garbage or what they would 'be willing' to pay, the truth is that high-mindedness often stops at the garbage can's rim" (*Rubbish!* by William Rathje and Cullen Murphy; HarperPerennial, page 45).

Each Tuesday morning my neighbors and I take part in an incredible act of magic. After carrying anywhere from one to three full trash cans to the curb, we climb into our cars and drive to our places of work. When we return home in the evening, we go back and look into the trash cans. *Voila!* The cans are empty! Someone reached into the cans and pulled out the trash. The garbage is soon replaced, however, and the magic act is repeated again the next week.

Throughout history people have used four techniques to deal with waste management issues:

(1) dumping
(2) burning
(3) source reduction
(4) recycling.

Each day the average citizen in the United States "throws away" about six pounds of trash. Paper makes up about forty percent of this waste. Have you ever wondered where "away" really is? Communities all across the United States are facing a growing problem with finding locations that can be designated as "away."

There is no shortage of space that could be used to put solid waste, but there is a shortage of people who are willing to have this waste discarded near them. Everyone claims the right to dispose of unwanted objects; but nobody wants those unwanted objects to be transported or deposited near where they live.

Don't Put Your Dust in My Dustpan

Don't put your dust in my dustpan,
My dustpan, my dustpan!
Don't put your dust in my dustpan, my dustpan's full!

If you substitute *landfill* for *dustpan*, this camp song hints at a phenomenon—*the NIMBY Syndrome*—that is spreading across the United States. NIMBY stands for "Not In My Back Yard." NIMBY describes the efforts of community groups to keep facilities with reputations for poor environmental policies from locating in or near their neighborhoods. Landfills, quarries, hazardous waste plants, and some industries are among those targeted by NIMBY.

DISCUSSION POINT

What examples of "NIMBY" have you seen at work in your community or county?

What news stories have you read or heard in which "NIMBY" has been a factor?

What do you think of the term, environmental racism?

What examples of environmental racism can you think of in your community, county, or state?

Communities that are well organized and have political clout usually win in a struggle to keep an unwanted facility out of their neighborhood. Low-income and racial minority communities that are poorly organized and have little political clout are often the losers. This pattern seems to be widespread. Some persons have labelled this phenomenon, "environmental racism."

The "NIMBY coat" is used as a prop in school recycling programs at the Cumberland Science Museum in Nashville, Tennessee. Using a lab coat covered with sections of Velcro, staff members wear discarded solid waste. This NIMBY coat helps them explain problems that take place when we generate solid waste, but no one is willing to have a landfill located near them.

WRITTEN REFLECTION

Write down personal responses to these questions; then discuss them in your group.

How many pounds of trash do you think you throw away each day?

Describe ways in which you could reduce the volume of trash you send to the landfill.

Which of the four techniques for waste management (dumping, burning, source reduction, and recycling) do you use? Which of these techniques do you prefer?

In what type of neighborhood or area is the landfill or incinerator for your community located?

Does it fit the pattern of placing such facilities in the backyards of those with the least amount of power to oppose them?

How would you respond if a landfill, an incinerator, or a waste transfer station was being proposed for your neighborhood?

If you would not want the proposed facility in your neighborhood, in what location should it be placed?

May the Circle Be Unbroken!

Since 1971 the University of Arizona, through the Garbage Project, has been using the tools of archaeology to answer serious questions about human behavior in modern society. Staff members of this effort, which has become known as "garbology," have searched through more than 250,000 pounds of garbage from trash cans and landfills. This effort has unearthed fascinating information about our treatment of solid waste.

The most important lesson. . . is the importance of market forces as the power plant of recycling. Money powers recycling as surely as the sun's energy powers the winds; absent the money, and recycling lies becalmed. The popular image of what constitutes recycling—separating one's garbage into various categories, leaving it neatly sorted at curbside, and seeing it carted off by industrious sanitation workers—does not really constitute recycling at all. It constitutes *sorting* and *collecting*. Recycling has not occurred until the loop is closed: that is, until someone buys (or gets paid to take) the sorted materials, manufactures them into something else, and sells that something back to the public (*Rubbish!*, page 203).

Natural cycles, such as the water cycle, help us understand the processes of recycling. The most important lesson is that we do not truly recycle until products go through the entire cycle of *purchase, utilization, collection and sorting, reprocessing, production, and repurchase.*

In New Jersey, legislation went into force in 1987 requiring that every community in the state begin to set aside, for the purposes of recycling, any three commonly discarded commodities: for example, aluminum cans, PET bottles, and newspapers. At the time, New Jersey was already collecting 50 percent of its newspapers (the national average today is about 33 percent), but within a few months of the law's taking effect the proportion of all newspapers being collected had soared to 62 percent, and the price of newsprint had fallen from $45 per ton to minus $25 per ton. In other words recyclers had to pay someone to take the newspapers away (possibly to a warehouse; possibly to a landfill). What happened in New Jersey happened to towns and cities throughout the Northeast. As mandated collection programs continued coming on line, the ripple effects began to spread further afield. Even if the economics are not sometimes disastrous, there simply are not enough mills in the United States to process all of the paper being collected here, and some paper companies have proved gun-shy about making the $500 million investment that each new paper-recycling mill requires, or even the $40 to $60 million investment that the retrofitting of existing facilities would entail. Retrofitting also takes a lot of time: four to six years (*Rubbish!*, pages 206-7).

For many years church youth groups, scout troops, and schools have raised money by collecting, sorting, and selling items such as newspaper, aluminum cans, and glass. In most cases, however, these groups have made few attempts to purchase recycled products that "close the loop" that leads to true recycling.

WRITTEN REFLECTION

Write your responses to these questions as you consider ways in which you can help to close the loop of recycling.

In what ways and to what extent have you sought to collect, sort, and sell recyclable materials?

In what ways can you personally and/or as a group increase the amount of recycled and recyclable materials that are purchased in your homes, churches, and places of work?

In *Rubbish!* it is estimated that an investment of between $40 to $60 million would be required to equip an existing paper mill for recycling (*Rubbish!*, page 207). To what extent would you be willing to make personal or church investments that support such a project?

DISCUSSION POINT

Allow time for persons to discuss their written reflections in smaller groups and/or in the larger group.

Ten Commandments of Waste Management

The authors of the book, *Rubbish!*, offer ten commandments for waste management.

1. Don't think of our garbage problems in terms of a crisis.

2. Don't bow before false panaceas.

3. Be willing to pay for garbage disposal.

DISCUSSION POINT

Ask the group members to discuss these ten commandments, starting with these questions:

To what extent do you agree or disagree with each "commandment"?

To what extent do you think particular "commandments" are defensible on religious grounds?

FOR NEXT TIME

WORSHIP

After sharing prayer concerns among members of the group, close with this prayer or another one in your own words.

4. Use money as a behavioral incentive.

5. Distrust symbolic targets.

6. Focus on the big-ticket items.

7. Buy recycled and recyclable products.

8. Encourage modest changes in household behavior.

9. Be responsible about risk.

10. Educate the next generation—without the myths (pages 238-245).

During the coming week, try becoming aware of what you do with the things you do not need or want. Think about how you handle your trash and garbage: Where does it go once it leaves your house? Also think about what "commandments" you would add to the above list as you try to think about your waste management specifically as a Christian.

Write prayer concerns of group members here:

Gracious God: we are aware that you have entrusted us with varying amounts of goods. We confess that we do not always use them to their fullest. Help us to be wise in the ways we use and dispose of the things entrusted to us. In Jesus' name we pray. Amen.

CHAPTER FOUR

WE ARE ONE IN THE SPIRIT

CHECKING IN

Before you start to look at the material for this session, be sure to take time for group members to bring each other up to date on what has been happening in their lives. Also, ask if persons have anything to share in the way of new learnings related to the environment, or if they want to talk about any of the "Before Next Time" activities suggested in previous weeks.

DISCUSSION POINT

What does it mean to be an "effective steward?"

"Now the whole group of those who believed were of one heart and soul, and no one claimed private ownership of any possessions, but everything they owned was held in common. With great power the apostles gave their testimony to the resurrection of the Lord Jesus, and great grace was upon them all. There was not a needy person among them, for as many as owned lands or houses sold them and brought the proceeds of what was sold. They laid it at the apostles' feet, and it was distributed to each as any had need" (Acts 4:32-35).

Our national park system was developed so that citizens of current and future generations would have the opportunity to experience the awe-inspiring beauty of these natural treasures. When we visit a national park, we usually receive instructions that we should leave the park in the same condition in which we found it. This is often communicated through the use of signs. One of my favorite signs for communicating this message for stewardship of the land reads, "Take only photos; Leave only footprints!"

As human influence spreads to every part of the globe, and even into travel beyond Earth's atmosphere, it has become clear that we must extend this message of stewardship to all parts of God's creation. As a world society, we are involved in intense discussions about how we can devise proper and just systems for preserving, conserving, and managing the resources that God has entrusted to us for our care and use.

In this session, we will explore ways in which we can reorganize our lives to be more effective stewards of God's creation.

Take Only Photos; Leave Only Footprints

"The basis of humankind's spiritual and social well-being is acceptance of the fact that 'the earth is the LORD'S and the fullness thereof' (Psalm 24:1). When we accept with humility and gratitude this fundamental biblical truth, we open up the possibility of authentic faith and responsible stewardship. As sons and daughters of God we are to be loving stewards of creation. This call goes beyond responsible stewardship of our possessions; we have no ultimate claim to ownership of anything. The resources of the earth are God's gift to present and future generations and are to be used to bless the whole family" (Jack A. Nelson, *Sojourners*, June, 1979).

Even in the national parks, a preservation message is difficult to maintain. Park vandalism, encroachment of air pollution within and from outside the parks, and traffic and business developments that result from heavy park visitation act together with other forces to cause deterioration of the natural beauty of the parks. These issues are raised often in discussions about management priorities of the national park system.

DISCUSSION POINT

Ask group members to discuss their reflections to this question.

Preservation, conservation, and management issues become even more complex when we extend them to areas outside of the park system. Reflect on your understanding of our responsibility to leave the earth for future generations. Do you accept the concept that we have no claim to ownership of the land?

Let's Make a Deal

"As I understand it, what economists mean by "market forces" are (1) the manufacturer's pursuit of high profits, and (2) the shopper's pursuit of low prices. Heaven knows these things are good for manufacturers and shoppers. And most religious environmentalists will cheerfully agree market forces should be given a fair amount of freedom in most areas.

"But there are parts of our planet's ecosystem whose importance far outranks the needs of the marketplace—because these things provide benefits that we need much more than we need cheap goods. Some examples: a healthy ozone layer, a stable climate for agriculture, productive topsoils, durable food crop species, clean air and water, places of unusual beauty—and healthy, resilient wild ecosystems to keep as biological reserves" (Marshall Massey, "Befriending Creation"; Friends Committee on Unity with Nature, February 1993; pages 2-3).

Usually the price of a product is influenced by its cost of production and the amount of demand that is present from consumers. One of the difficulties with using a market force approach to environmental concerns is that society has not established a monetary value for clean air, clean water, a stable climate, and other environmental factors that are used as resources in the process of manufacturing products. Even though these characteristics of the natural environment are valued by many, they are assigned no monetary value when the cost of production is calculated. This leads to a distortion of the market. Because most of us have been trained to take great pride in our ability to find a good deal, this distortion benefits each of us as we seek to accumulate more things at the lowest price possible.

Even though it is easy to accuse irresponsible companies of abusing the environment, each of us bears some responsibility for the policies that our businesses, government, and even households have pursued.

If we are to correct these distortions in our personal lifestyles and the lifestyles of the institutions on which we depend, we will need to search our actions carefully to identify places where we can be more faithful stewards of creation. This endeavor requires personal commitment. It also requires mutual support, cooperation and accountability from others who seek appropriate responses to questions of environmental responsibility. While confrontation is sometimes appropriate to highlight an issue, it is often difficult to place complete blame on one source.

"We need to resist the tendency to pit jobs versus environment, workers versus management, loggers versus owls. . . . We need to become less concerned with squelching others' arguments and more with reaching beyond anger to the human beings behind it. 'Those who take a confrontational approach,' says Amory Lovins, 'tend to see companies and governments as monolithic. The truth is, all organizations are made up of people.' I'd like to see us keep that in mind, and approach those people in a spirit of truth and peace" (Chris Lansing, "Befriending Creation," February 1993; page 3).

WRITTEN REFLECTION

Provide enough time for persons to work through these written reflections individually.

Think about specific ways that you personally could improve your care of the environment. Write your reflections in the space below:

(1) List some ways that you could change activities in your home that would make it more earth friendly.

(2) List some ways that you could change activities in your church that would make it more earth friendly.

(3) List some ways that you could change activities in your work place that would make it more earth friendly.

(4) List some ways that you could change your shopping habits that would make them more earth friendly.

(5) List some ways that you could change the purchasing practices of your church or work place that would make them more earth friendly.

(6) Describe ways that you could invest in technologies that would create new markets for recycled goods.

(7) Describe ways that you could influence your church or work place to invest in technologies that would create new markets for recycled goods.

(8) Describe situations in which you believe confrontation may be the most appropriate response to bring about changes that would improve environmental quality.

GROUP INTERACTION

Divide the larger group into smaller groups of no more than four persons. Ask smaller groups to share ideas for each of the ten written reflections. Invite persons in smaller groups to consider two or three items to which they would be willing to commit themselves.

(9) Describe situations in which you believe negotiation may be the most appropriate response to bring about changes that would improve environmental quality.

(10) List some land-use policies that your community could adopt that would make it more earth friendly.

Imagine that you have been given the power to place a monetary value on items such as clean water, clean air, species extinction, habitat destruction, or places of unusual beauty. <u>How much value would you establish for each of them? Do you think it would be wise to try to establish such a pricing system?</u>

Ask the same smaller groups to work through the instructions in the main text.

BIBLE STUDY

Now Hear the Word of the Lord!

"Then the LORD appeared to Solomon in the night and said to him: 'I have heard your prayer, and have chosen this place for myself as a house of sacrifice. When I shut up the heavens so that there is no rain, or command the locust to devour the land, or send pestilence among my people, if my people who are called by my name humble themselves, pray, seek my face, and turn from their wicked ways, then I will hear from heaven, and will forgive their sin and heal their land. Now my eyes will be open and my ears attentive to the prayer that is made in this place. For now I have chosen and consecrated this house so that my name may be there forever; my eyes and my heart will be there for all time' " (2 Chronicles 7:12-16).

DISCUSSION POINT

In addition to discussing the question in the main text, you may want to ask the larger group or smaller groups to rewrite this passage as if God were speaking about the environment to American Christians today.

WORSHIP

Plan ahead and ask different LIFESEARCH group members to lead different portions of this worship service.

Think about this Bible passage from 2 Chronicles. In the context of 2 Chronicles, King Solomon of Israel has just built and consecrated the sanctuary of the new Temple in Jerusalem. <u>In this passage, God speaks to Solomon in the night with words of warning as well as words of hope. In what language might God speak to you and to the church within the context of what is happening to the environment?</u>

This worship service offers an opportunity to reflect on the discussions you have had during the time you have met as a LIFESEARCH group. You have explored your relationship with the earth and with the earth's resources and people. Through this worship, listen for God's word of forgiveness and God's desire to remain in covenant with all generations of humanity. You will be challenged to look at your personal lifestyle in relation to the earth's limited resources, the needs of others, and the impact of our actions or inactions upon the world community.

Leader: We will now take time to reflect upon our own attitudes and actions towards the environment. Let us think about our relationship to the earth and its people. How do we relate to the earth, to the air, to the fruits of the earth? Do we use or abuse them? How can we advocate proper use of the earth and its resources?

Scripture Lesson: Read Psalm 103:15-18

Time for Silent Prayer, Confession, and Commitment

Invite group members to share what commitments they might want to make concerning their care of the environment.

Response: God has promised to be with us, and we are not alone in our journey to be faithful stewards of God's creation. We are assured of our relationship with God by the following words:

"Then I saw a new heaven and a new earth; for the first heaven and the first earth had passed away. . . .And I heard a loud voice from the throne saying,
    'See, the home of God is among mortals.
    He will dwell with them as their God;
    they will be his peoples,
    and God himself will be with them;
    he will wipe every tear from their eyes.

Death will be no more;
mourning and crying and pain will be no more,
for the first things have passed away.'
And the one who was seated on the throne said, 'See, I am
making all things new' " (Revelation 21:1, 3-5).

Leader: Now more than ever before, we are aware of our interdependence with all people everywhere and of our responsibility to assure the just distribution of resources in the global community. The world is an altar on which our lives are offered to God in worship and to each other in love and service. Go in peace to walk softly on the earth and to be messengers of peace for all of creation.

(Adapted from *World Day of Prayer*, 1981 Leader's Guide; Church Women United, 1980)

CHAPTER FIVE

CALMING THE STORM!

CHECKING IN

Begin this session by inviting anyone to share significant events that may have occurred in their lives since last time.

Images of Destruction

"Hear this, O elders,
    give ear, all inhabitants of the land!
Has such a thing happened in your days,
    or in the days of your ancestors?
Tell your children of it,
    and let your children tell their children,
    and their children another generation" (Joel 1:2-3).

"To you, O Lord, I cry.
For fire has devoured
    the pastures of the wilderness,
and flames have burned
    all the trees of the field.
Even the wild animals cry to you
    because the watercourses are dried up,
and fire has devoured the pastures of the wilderness" (1:19-20).

"Let all the inhabitants of the land tremble,
    for the day of the Lord is coming, it is near—" (2:1b).

"Fire devours in front of them,
    and behind them a flame burns.
Before them the land is like the garden of Eden,
    but after them is a desolate wilderness,
    and nothing escapes them" (2:3).

WORSHIP

Begin by praying this prayer:

Send me, Lord, as an evangel of home and security to those whose paths will cross with mine this day. Amen.

(From *A Guide to Prayer for All God's People*, by Rueben P. Job and Norman Shawchuck; Upper Room Books, 1990; page 253.)

DISCUSSION POINT

What natural disasters today make an impact on whole nations as did the plague of locusts?

An invasion of locusts caused the disaster described by Joel. A nation mourned loss of agricultural bounty as locusts quickly devastated grain fields and orchards. With sudden ferociousness the "good," symbolized by productive fields and orchards, was disrupted by evil. Distress—even death—was the inevitable result. To Joel, the locust attack was merely a warning of an oncoming day of the Lord when sin would be punished.

These images of destruction, however ancient, are similar to other disasters, such as those caused by the misuse of pesticides, the strip mining of coal, the use of defoliants in war, the eruption of a volcano, or the violence of an earthquake.

Each year thousands of people become victims of natural disasters. Today there are about 500 active volcanoes around the world. Since 1904, people have reported feeling an average of more than 150,000 earthquakes per year, and some seismologists have estimated that between 1 million and 2 million earthquakes take place annually. In addition, people face the destruction of numerous floods, landslides, tornadoes, monsoons, hurricanes, thunderstorms, droughts, and other potentially catastrophic natural events.

In this session we will explore how we view the relationship between God and humanity during times of natural disaster. We will also investigate common perceptions about natural disasters and explore differences in how wealthy and poor societies affect and are affected by natural disasters.

Story Time

"The word *disaster* comes from a Latin phrase meaning 'ill-starred,' or the 'product of unhappy fate.' This reflects the way people around the world still think of the disasters that threaten them. Although unfortunate and even tragic, disasters are impersonal and inevitable, and there is little to gain from worrying about them. Medieval scholars tried to depict disasters as the result of God's wrath, like dress rehearsals for Judgment Day. Later, it was fashionable to consider them subversions of the otherwise symmetrical natural order of the universe. Most people, however, continued to believe that disasters were written in the stars.

"Disasters interest us on many levels, from morbid fascination to dispassionate scientific study. The awesome strength that nature is able to muster so casually serves to remind us of our own fragility and of the transience of life on earth. Sometimes we need to be reminded" (*Natural Disasters*, Michael Friedman Publishing Group, 1990; pages 9,10).

WRITTEN REFLECTION

After everyone completes this task, share your responses.

Some people refer to natural disasters as "acts of God." Do you think they are "acts of God"? If so, how do you reconcile that view with the perception of a loving and caring God? Use the space below to respond. Describe natural disasters you or people you know have experienced.

Act of God or Acts of Humankind

Because the great Midwest floods of 1993 occurred during intense debate on priorities of the federal budget, new questions were raised about government's responsibility to assist victims of natural disasters. While the world marveled at the community spirit, heroism, and perseverance of flood victims, concerns were raised about whether this disaster was an "act of God" caused by natural forces or an act of humankind.

The great Midwest flood of 1993 was a natural disaster. Human behavior, however, contributed heavily to the record flood levels and the tremendous financial losses. The level of water that travels through rivers fluctuates with time. By using erosion to carve their signature into the land forms that they leave behind, however, rivers usually provide clear evidence about the amount of space that they need for their flood plain.

When people decide to move into the floodplain of a river, they assume a risk that the level of the river will never again need the same amount of space that it needed previously. Attempts to place rivers into a container through flood-protection efforts such as dams, dikes, levees, and channel modifications give people confidence that the risk they face is minimal.

Most channel modifications, however, are temporary solutions that are changed by the river through sediment deposits and new plant growth. They need to be maintained regularly or flood protection will be lost.

The potential for tremendous problems is created when large numbers of people create expensive developments in the floodplain with the assumption that no risk exists. They usually assume that the government will protect them from flooding or "it could never happen" to them.

DISCUSSION POINT

In the context of the 1993 Midwest flood and other recent natural disasters, what do you think about the statement that "we lack adequate respect for and understanding of our natural environment to take steps to prevent future disasters"?

Just as we can expect a mess when we attempt to put too much water into a water balloon, we should also expect a disaster when we try to contain a river in a floodplain that is too small. As television news reports demonstrated repeatedly during the summer of 1993, disastrous losses of life and property usually happen quickly when the floodwaters break through a levee.

For many years, the causes and effects of the great Midwest flood of 1993 will be studied and discussed. No single group was responsible for this disaster. The size of the flood, however, was increased dramatically by the cumulative activities of all of those who occupied or restricted the size of the flood plain. Perhaps one of the greatest tragedies of this disaster is that we lack adequate respect for and understanding of our natural environment to take steps to prevent future disasters. In a sense, the flood of 1993 was predicted through this description of a flood that occurred twenty years earlier:

"The Mississippi River remained above flood stage for seventy-seven days at St. Louis; ninety-seven days at Chester, Illinois; sixty-three days at Memphis, Tennessee; and eighty-eight days at Vicksburg, Mississippi. . . . Although the dikes and levees along the Mississippi River are designed to provide flood protection, the channel construction that has accompanied the building of levees actually made a big flood out of a moderate one in 1973 by increasing the river stage or elevation. Although river levels during the flood topped a 189-year record, and was, therefore, reported by the news media as a 200-year flood, the discharge volume was only equivalent to a 30-year event. The confinement of the river by levees and various navigation works has reduced the channel

cross-section and prevented overflow onto the flood plain."
The 1973 flood's record was thus human made.

(*Geologic Hazards*, Resources and Environmental Planning; by Griggs and Gilchrist; Wadsworth Publishing Company; page 308.)

GROUP INTERACTION

If your group is larger than eight members, split into smaller groups of four to six persons to undertake this simulation activity.

DISCUSSION POINT

If you split into more than one group to do this simulation activity, be sure to take time to discuss findings together in the whole group.

Your group is a commission that is responsible for making decisions about the redevelopment of the flood area. A team of scientists has recommended that one town be relocated to a nearby area that is outside of the flood plain. The site of the existing town would be used for farming, with the understanding that it will be used as an overflow area during future floods. Residents of the town, which has been in existence for 150 years, are violently opposed to this plan. You have the power to make the final decision in this matter. You also control financial resources that could pay for redevelopment of the town in its current site, relocation to a new site, and payment for use of the land as a flood overflow area. What would you decide? Be prepared to discuss your reasons.

Tale of Two Earthquakes!

During our early history, humans survived daily life-threatening encounters with natural events. Human losses from natural disasters affected relatively few people, however. Most people were mobile because of their nomadic lifestyle, and very few lived in urban centers. People began to suffer greater losses as they adopted more settled lifestyles and as urban centers were developed in high-risk areas.

Scientific efforts to predict earthquakes and many other natural disasters are still in their infancy. Methods of predicting events such as hurricanes and floods, however, have reached a high level of sophistication and success. Use of this ability to predict and to issue warnings about potential disasters has been credited with saving lives and property. Sometimes entire communities have time to evacuate and to move valuable possessions to a protected environment. Scientists have also developed methods of identifying regions most likely to suffer natural disasters.

Planners and engineers in wealthy countries use this information to choose locations and adapt construction methods for new types of development. While financial losses from natural disasters continue to rise each year because of an increase in the number and concentration of buildings, the death toll from natural disasters has declined steadily for several years.

As the human population has grown and become more concentrated in urban centers in developing countries, however, the financial toll and number of fatalities from these natural forces has continued to increase significantly.

It is customary to rate the size of an earthquake with the Richter scale, which is based on the amount of energy that it releases. While this is an important tool for understanding earthquakes, it does not necessarily give an indication of the loss of life and property. For example, the September, 1993 earthquake in India measured only 6.4 on the Richter scale, while the October, 1989 earthquake in San Francisco measured 6.9. The loss of human life in San Francisco was very small, however, compared to the tens of thousands who lost their lives in India.

GROUP INTERACTION

Using the same groups involved in the previous simulation activity, follow the instructions for this simulation activity.

The loss of human life is dependent on the size of the earthquake, the type and condition of the structures, and the number of people who are present at the time of the event. Many victims in India were trapped in buildings that were designed to provide basic shelter and were not designed to withstand the forces of an earthquake. Also, the living spaces were near the places where people work. In San Francisco, however, most buildings and other structures were designed to withstand the forces of a major earthquake. Many of the fatalities were related to the collapse of a section of the highway system. Because of the timing of the earthquake, however, many were spared from death due to the travel schedules of suburban dwellers who have a nomadic lifestyle of commuting between their work and residences.

Imagine that you are a member of a special United Nations team that is investigating methods for improving the quality of life for thousands of people who are living on the side of a mountain in Peru. Your mission is to develop a plan for the health care, safety, and economic development of those who live in this region. Most of the houses are poorly constructed and offer only basic shelter. This area is near a fault, and seismologists suspect that it could suffer a major earthquake within the next few years. Residents of this region struggle each day to secure the basic necessities for staying alive, and they do not have the resources to prepare for such an earthquake. They view earthquakes as "acts of God" over which they have no control, but each October they celebrate a special religious festival which they hope will help to protect them from suffering an earthquake that year.

WRITTEN REFLECTION

List all of the options that you can think of that could help the people in this region to avoid the destruction of the earthquake that you suspect will come within the next few years.

If you have more than one smaller group working on this simulation, be sure to take time to discuss findings together in the larger group.

Make your list on chalkboard or newsprint so that group members can easily read it. After you list these options, discuss each one of them and imagine that an outside consulting group has come into your community and made the same suggestions for your region. Discuss ways you would like to improve environmental quality if they didn't require drastic changes in your lifestyle.

BEFORE NEXT TIME

Next time you will explore your views on recycling. In preparation, research your community's garbage problem. Is there a recycling station near you? Where is the nearest one? How does recycling benefit your community?

WORSHIP

In closing, you may want to read or sing the words to this hymn.

> *O God, our help in ages past,*
> *our hope for years to come;*
> *our shelter from the stormy blast,*
> *and our eternal home!*
>
> *Under the shadow of thy throne,*
> *still may we dwell secure;*
> *sufficient is thine arm alone,*
> *and our defense is sure.*
>
> *Before the hills in order stood,*
> *or earth received her frame,*
> *from everlasting, thou art God,*
> *to endless years the same.*
>
> *O God, our help in ages past,*
> *our hope for years to come;*
> *be thou our guide while life shall last,*
> *and our eternal home.*
> *Isaac Watts, 1719 (Psalm 90)*

Pray this week for persons throughout the world who suffer from earthquakes, floods and other disasters.

CHAPTER SIX

NEW WINE/OLD WINE SKINS

CHECKING IN

Before you begin this session, make sure you take time to have group members share what has happened in their lives since the last time you met together. Ask persons also to share about work they have done on "Before Next Time" activities from the previous session, or about any new insights they have had concerning the environment.

"Then the disciples of John came to him, saying, 'Why do we and the Pharisees fast often, but your disciples do not fast?' And Jesus said to them, . . .'No one sews a piece of unshrunk cloth on an old cloak, for the patch pulls away from the cloak, and a worse tear is made. Neither is new wine put into old wineskins; otherwise, the skins burst, and the wine is spilled, and the skins are destroyed; but new wine is put into fresh wineskins, and so both are preserved' " (Matthew 9:14-17).

In the early morning of February 26, 1972, residents in the Buffalo Creek valley of West Virginia were awakened by a series of explosions stemming from the collapse of a five hundred foot pile of mine waste that had been used to create a makeshift dam. Mine workers, who were changing shifts at the time, watched helplessly as mud, rock, and sludge erupted three hundred feet into the air. Because the telephone lines were quickly destroyed, witnesses were unable to warn residents downstream of the coming disaster.

"They could only watch as the water and sludge crested over the top of the exploding gop pile and burst into the valley, 'boiling up like dry flour when you pour water on it.'

"The flood traveled at first at a speed of at least 30 miles an hour—in a solid wall 20 or 30 feet high. People who saw it coming as they headed up the Buffalo Creek road barely had time to throw their cars into reverse, turn around wherever there was room, and head back downstream, leaning on their horns, flashing their lights, trying to warn other people who had heard the explosions but still did not know what was happening. There was very little time to do anything. It takes a few seconds to collect your wits when you see a wall of water bearing down on you, especially when you live in a valley where there are only a few exits—hollows running at right angles to the main valley. For most of the people who died, it was like being in the barrel of a gun and seeing the bullet coming. There was nowhere to go" (*The Pittston Mentality: Manslaughter on Buffalo Creek*, by Thomas N. Bethell and Davitt McAteer; Appalachian Movement Press, Inc., 1972; pages 21-22).

More than 125 people were killed in this flash flood. There were nearly 5,000 survivors, but entire towns were washed away. Approximately 1,000 families lost their houses and possessions.

The mining company initially blamed the disaster on an "act of God." Residents of Buffalo Creek were onraged by this claim. They accused the company of lying about God. After extensive investigation, they exposed the actions of the coal company that had led to this disaster.

DISCUSSION POINT

What do you think about the term "act of God?"

Although the disaster at Buffalo Creek happened more than twenty years ago, this case highlights several issues that continue today. Problems still exist concerning the disposal of obsolete, unusable, and sometimes hazardous materials. For example, most disasters are characterized as being "acts of God." This phrase should be understood as a legal term that is used to avoid liability, rather than a theological stance.

At Buffalo Creek, a government inspector had cited the mine operation for violating a law because the dam did not have a spillway. A properly placed spillway might have saved the dam. A representative of the coal company explained that the mining operation would have had to close for the period of time a spillway was under construction. This loss of production time would have reduced revenue for the company and caused the temporary loss of ninety jobs.

The coal company chose not to comply with the spillway law. Coal extraction and jobs were considered to be more urgent than environmental and safety precautions. When asked why the company had violated Federal Coal Mine Health and Safety Act standards by using mine refuse to impound water at the dam, the company's response was, "We had no other place to dump it" (*The Buffalo Creek Disaster*, by Gerald M. Stern; Vintage, 1977; page 163).

Investigations also discovered that coal company employees monitored the dam hourly throughout the morning of the disaster. They were concerned that the dam could fail, but they did not issue a warning so that the valley could be evacuated.

DISCUSSION POINT

Did the residents of Buffalo Creek have the right to know about this situation? What do we do with waste products, obsolete technologies, banned pesticides, nuclear wastes, and other substances that have been declared to be unsafe in this country?

Some hazardous waste is destroyed or recycled. Other such materials are exported to countries that do not have the same environmental restrictions. Some hazardous waste has been buried or dumped because there is no other place to put it. Most hazardous material disposal methods have been inadequate. Leaks into the environment are frequent. Then there are the stories of catastrophic events such as Buffalo Creek and Love Canal.

DISCUSSION POINT

What are your thoughts and feelings about these questions at this time?

Are high profits and job security more important than a safe environment for a business' workers and neighbors? Do the neighbors of a business have the right to know of the presence of situations that have the potential for causing severe problems?

In this session, we will explore these issues and potential responses by the church.

Did You Know?

"The question of which came first, the chicken or the egg, has now been answered by the study of evolution. The egg came first, for birds are the descendants of egg-laying scaly reptiles.

"The question of which will succumb first, the bird or its egg, remains open. Will the oystercatcher die from the effects of oil pollution before or after its eggs have been finally sterilized by poisonous chemicals tipped into the oceans?" (*Save the Birds*, by Shreiber, Diamond, Peterson, and Cronkite; Houghton Mifflin, 1987; pages 2-3).

Until the 1940's farmers used a mixture of biological, chemical, and mechanical methods to control insects that affected their crops. DDT was one the first pesticides to be used widely to control insects. It affected a wide variety of species, saved application time because it stayed in the environment for a long time, was relatively inexpensive, and was safer than other available chemicals such as arsenic, cyanide, and heavy metals. It was widely used in the United States until it was banned in the early 1970's.

"During the 1960's, scientists were alarmed to discover an ever-increasing number of Peregrine, Sparrowhawk, and Golden Eagle nests containing broken or malformed eggs. Further research then showed that more than twenty bird species across Europe and North America were suffering similar disastrous breeding failures.

"The birds were all birds of prey or predatory water birds occupying the top levels in their food chains. All showed high levels of DDT contamination, which was causing the hen birds to lay eggs with shells too thin to take the weight of the incubating adult.

"Worldwide investigations proved the link beyond argument against the use of this most persistent chemical agent. In areas where DDT is no longer used, the affected birds are now, slowly, showing some signs of recovery" (*Save the Birds*, page 300).

Substances that have been banned in the United States such as DDT, are often exported for use in other countries. Many such substances are marketed and subsidized heavily for use in developing countries. Bird populations in many of these countries are facing the same problem identified in North America and Europe in the 1960's.

Many farmers around the world have found success in using Integrated Pest Management (IPM). IPM utilizes an ecosystem approach to control insects, involving special planting techniques, genetic manipulation of crops planted, reintroduction of natural enemies, and limited chemical use.

Tasty but Toxic

When government import inspectors in Dallas opened up a shipment of cabbages from Mexico. . . they smelled insecticide. As is routine, the officials took a sample for laboratory analysis and let the rest continue on to market. Then the verdict came in. The cabbages contained illegal levels of BHC. . . . By the time the Dallas inspectors received news of the contamination, the cabbages were in supermarkets, refrigerators—and stomachs. No alert was issued. Except for an obscure reference in a government report sometime later, the public had no way of knowing the incident had occurred" (*Pro-Earth*; Friendship Press, 1985; page 40).

Imagine that you are part of the staff of a government agency responsible for inspecting and testing produce to ensure its safety for consumption. You have just learned about the situation described above.

Most of the food has already been distributed. Little can be done to correct the immediate situation. Some staff members recommend that no action be taken. They fear the public will lose confidence in your agency. They also worry that public disclosure could be devastating for the supermarket chain involved. It is one of the largest employers in your region.

GROUP INTERACTION

Divide your LIFESEARCH group into smaller groups of four or five persons. Ask them to read through and follow the simulation activity instructions in the main text. After smaller groups have had an opportunity to discuss together the "Discussion Point" questions in the main text, take time also to share reflections within the whole group.

Others on the staff feel that your agency should make every effort to retrieve any of the produce in question. They also want to take steps to ensure that this will never occur again. They are concerned that the public will be upset that their agency was not able to prevent human consumption of the cabbage, yet they also feel that the public will understand the mistake if assured about changes in future procedure.

Reflect on this situation and then discuss how you would respond. Be sure to deal with the following questions:

DISCUSSION POINT

What actions would you take if you were placed in this situation?

Do you think the public has a right to know when environmental hazards are present near the places where they live and work?

Do you think that United States companies should be able to export products to developing countries after those products have been banned in this country?

How Should We Respond?

"Half a century after the world's nuclear industries began accumulating radioactive waste, not a single one of the more than twenty-five countries producing nuclear power has found a safe, permanent way to dispose of it. Nuclear waste remains dangerous for hundreds of thousands of years— meaning that in producing it, today's governments assume responsibility for the fate of thousands of future generations.

"Geologic disposal . . . as with any human contrivance meant to last thousands of years, is little more than a calculated risk. Scientists still heatedly debate the possibility of disturbance of the waste by ground water, geological activity, or human intervention.

"Government officials frequently suggest that the waste issue has been solved in other countries. Yet no nation has developed a proven method of containing radioactive waste permanently. By their own timetables, in fact, most governments have found their efforts to bury waste moving in reverse" (*Vital Signs 1992*, by Brown, Flavin, & Kane; W.W. Norton and Co., 1992; pages 100-101).

News stories have reported the problems associated with cleanup efforts for hazardous waste disposal, nuclear waste disposal and nuclear weapon production sites. As the United States decommissions and abandons the first nuclear power plants and nuclear weapon production sites, our generation leaves future generations with a huge bill for cleanup operations. We also put our faith—rightly or wrongly—in the ability of future generations to discover technological and political solutions that we have not found. We also leave behind the potential for many more disasters.

BIBLE STUDY

Divide the larger group into two smaller groups. Assign Exodus 20:4-6 to one of the groups and Matthew 7:12 to the other group. Ask them to follow the instructions given in the main text.

Read Exodus 20:4-6. This passage is from the Ten Commandments and focuses on God's command not to commit idolatry. Spend at least three minutes silently reflecting upon this brief passage. Then consider these questions: <u>In what ways might idolatry (broadly understood) be involved in disasters such as the one that took place at Buffalo Creek? What do you think about the portion of the passage in which God threatened to punish violators of this command even to the third and fourth generation? How might that threat of punishment apply to environmental disasters?</u>

DISCUSSION POINT

Read Matthew 7:12. You will probably recognize this verse as a version of the Golden Rule. Spend at least three minutes silently reflecting upon this brief passage. Then consider these questions: <u>How might the Golden Rule apply to the environmental concerns you have been reading about? In what ways might the Golden Rule apply to environmental concerns connected with persons living hundreds and even thousands of miles away from you? In what ways might the Golden Rule apply to environmental concerns connected with persons living distant from you in time?</u>

DISCUSSION POINT

Is there a difference between ways we respond to a natural disaster and a human made disaster, such as the hazardous waste incident at Love Canal? If so, what differences are there?

"In natural disasters, volunteer organizations customarily provide important assistance for the victims. In the Niagara Falls metropolitan area, not one traditional helping group, except the church, responded to the Love Canal people. There was no rallying of Boy Scouts, Lions Club, or Rotary.

"In natural disaster, whole communities are often strengthened and drawn together with a positive public spirit as they aid the victims. But Love Canal resulted in a collapse of supportive structures. Victims were isolated from the community. No local politician championed their cause. Doctors were reluctant to treat them. The sanctuary found in the safety of the home was severely threatened. Two neighborhood schools were shut down almost at the outset" (*Pro-Earth*, page 60).

One reason for this difference in the response of relief groups is that natural disasters usually take place quickly, requiring immediate and temporary responses. Disasters like those at Love Canal, however, develop over a long period of time and require long-term commitments. <u>Can you think of other reasons for this difference?</u>

GROUP INTERACTION

Divide into the same smaller groups as used in the earlier simulation activity. Ask groups to follow this set of simulation activity instructions in the main text. After allowing time for the smaller groups to discuss the questions in the main text, share reflections within the whole group.

DISCUSSION POINT

WORSHIP

Before closing, take time to allow group members to share any concerns to be included in prayer.

Covenant to continue to pray for and with each other in the days to come. Consider ways in which you might continue to work on environmental issues in your individual lives or in your life together. Close by praying the Lord's Prayer together.

Imagine that you have just received notification that the place where you live needs to be evacuated immediately because it was built on top of a toxic waste site. The letter indicates that the area will be sealed and that you will not be able to return.

What questions would you have about the causes of this disaster?

What types of support would you expect from the church and from other social agencies?

Would you feel any different if this had been a natural disaster?

How would you, your church, and other organizations of which you are a member respond to victims of a nearby natural disaster? a natural disaster from another country? a disaster that is caused by human negligence? Are there any differences?

Write prayer concerns in the space below:

THE LIFESEARCH
GROUP EXPERIENCE

Every LIFESEARCH group will be different. Because your group is made up of unique individuals, your group's experience will also be unique. No other LIFESEARCH group will duplicate the dynamics, feelings, and adventures your group will encounter.

And yet as we planned LIFESEARCH, we had a certain vision in mind about what we hoped might happen as people came together to use a LIFESEARCH book for discussion and support around a common concern. Each LIFESEARCH book focuses on some life concern of adults within a Christian context over a six-session course. LIFESEARCH books have been designed to be easy to lead, to encourage group nurture, and to be biblically based and needs-oriented.

Each chapter in this LIFESEARCH book has been designed for use during a one and one-half hour group session. In each LIFESEARCH book, you will find
• times for group members to "check in" with each other concerning what has gone on in their lives during the past week and what they wish to share from the past week concerning the material covered in the group sessions;
• times for group members to "check in" about how they are doing as a group;
• substantial information/reflection/discussion segments, often utilizing methods such as case studies and simulation;
• Bible study segments;
• segments in which a specific skill or process is introduced, tried out, and/or suggested for use during the week to come;
• segments that help group participants practice supporting one another with the concerns being explored.

LIFESEARCH was not planned with the usual one hour Sunday school class in mind. If you intend to use LIFESEARCH with a Sunday school class, you will need to adapt it to the length of time you have available. Either plan to take more than one week to discuss each chapter or be less ambitious with what you aim to accomplish in a session's time.

LIFESEARCH was also not planned to be used in a therapy group, a sensitivity group, or an encounter group.

> A LIFESEARCH group is simply a group of persons who come together to struggle together from a Christian perspective with a common life concern.

No one is expected to be an expert on the topic. No one is expected to offer psychological insights into what is going on. However, we do hope that LIFESEARCH group members will offer one another support and Christian love.

We will count LIFESEARCH as successful if you find your way to thought-provoking discussions centered around information, insights, and helps providing aid for living everyday life as Christians.

You might find it helpful to see what we envisioned a sample LIFESEARCH group might experience. Keep in mind, however, that your experience might be quite different. Leave room for your creativity and uniqueness. Remain receptive to God's Spirit.

You sit in the living room of a friend from church for the second session of your LIFESEARCH group. Besides you and your host, four other persons are present, sitting on the sofa and overstuffed chairs. You, your host, your group leader, and one other are church members, although not all of you make it to church that regularly. The remaining two persons are neighbors of the leader. You chat while a light refreshment and beverage are served by the host.

Your leader offers a brief prayer, and then asks each of you to share what has been going on in your lives during the past week since you last met. One member shares about a spouse who had outpatient surgery. Several mention how hectic the week was with the usual work- and family-related demands. Prayer concerns and requests are noted.

This session begins with a written reflection. The leader draws your attention to a brief question in the beginning of the chapter you were assigned to read for today. Group members are asked to think about the question and write a short response.

While the leader records responses on a small chalkboard brought for that purpose, members take turns sharing something from their written reflections. A brief discussion follows when one group member mentions something she had never noticed before.

Group members respond as the leader asks for any reports concerning trying out the new life skill learned in the previous session. Chuckles, words of encouragement, and suggestions for developing the new skill further pepper the reports.

The leader notes one of the statements made in the assigned chapter from the LIFESEARCH book and asks to what extent the statement is true to the experience of the group members. Not much discussion happens on this point, since everyone agrees the statement is true. But one of the members presses on to the next statement in the LIFESEARCH book, and all sorts of conversation erupts! All six group members have their hot buttons pushed.

Your leader calls the group to move on to Bible study time. You read over the text, and then participate in a dramatic reading in which everyone has a part. During the discussion that follows the reading, you share some insights that strike you for the first time because you identify with the person whose role you read.

You and the other group members take turns simulating a simple technique suggested in the book for dealing with a specific concern. Everyone coaches everyone else; and what could have been an anxiety-producing experience had you remained so self-conscious, quickly becomes both fun and helpful. You and one of the other group members agree to phone each other during the week to find out how you're doing with practicing this technique in real life.

It's a few minutes later than the agreed upon time to end, but no one seems to mind. You read together a prayer printed at the end of this week's chapter.

On the way out to your car, you ponder how quickly the evening has passed. You feel good about what you've learned and about deepening some new friendships. You look forward to the next time your LIFESEARCH group meets.

This has been only one model of how a LIFESEARCH group session might turn out. Yours will be different. But as you give it a chance, you will learn some things and you will deepen some friendships. That's what you started LIFESEARCH for anyway, isn't it?

STARTING A LifeSearch GROUP

The key ingredient to starting a LifeSearch group is *interest*. People are more likely to get excited about those things in which they are interested. People are more likely to join a group to study and to work on those areas of their lives in which they are interested.

Interest often comes when there is some itch to be scratched in a person's life, some anxiety to be soothed, or some pain to be healed.

Are persons interested in the topic of a LifeSearch book? Or, perhaps more important to ask, do they have needs in their lives that can be addressed using a LifeSearch book?

If you already have an existing group that finds interesting one of the topics covered by the LifeSearch books, go for it! Just keep in mind that LifeSearch is intended more as a small-group resource than as a class study textbook.

If you want to start a new group around LifeSearch, you can begin in one of two ways:

- You can begin with a group of interested people and let them choose from among the topics LifeSearch offers; or

- You can begin with one of the LifeSearch topics and locate people who are interested in forming a group around that topic.

What is the right size for a LifeSearch group? Well, how many persons do you have who are interested?

Actually, LifeSearch is intended as a *small-group* resource. The best size is between four and eight persons. Under four persons will make it difficult to carry out some of the group interactions. Over eight and not everyone will have a good opportunity to participate. The larger the group means the less time each person has to share.

> **Interest often comes when there is some itch to be scratched in a person's life, some anxiety to be soothed, or some pain to be healed.**

If you have more than eight persons interested in your LifeSearch group, why not start two groups?

Or if you have a group larger than eight that just does not want to split up, then be sure to divide into smaller groups of no more than eight for discussion times. LifeSearch needs the kind of interaction and discussion that only happen in small groups.

How do you find out who is interested in LifeSearch? One good way is for you to sit down with a sheet of paper and list the names of persons whom you think might be interested. Even better would be for you to get one or two other people to brainstorm names with you. Then start asking. Call them on the telephone. Or visit them in person. People respond more readily to personal invitations.

When you invite persons and they seem interested in LIFESEARCH, ask them if they will commit to attending all six sessions. Emergencies do arise, of course. However, the group's life is enhanced if all members participate in all sessions.

LIFESEARCH is as much a group experience as it is a time for personal learning.

As you plan to begin a LIFESEARCH group, you will need to answer these questions:

- **Who will lead the group?** Will you be the leader for all sessions? Do you plan to rotate leadership among the group members? Do you need to recruit an individual to serve as group leader?

- **Where will you meet?** You don't have to meet at a church. In fact, if you are wanting to involve a number of persons not related to your church, a neutral site might be more appropriate. Why not hold your meetings at a home? But if you

do, make sure plans are made to hold distractions and interruptions to a minimum. Send the children elsewhere and put the answering machine on. Keep any refreshments simple.

- **How will you get the LIFESEARCH books to group members before the first session?** You want to encourage members to read the first chapter in advance of the first session. Do you need to have an initial gathering some days before the first discussion sessions in order to hand out books and take care of other housekeeping matters? Do you need to mail or otherwise transport the books to group members?

Most LIFESEARCH groups will last only long enough to work through the one LIFESEARCH book in which there is interest. Be open, however, to the possibility of either continuing your LIFESEARCH group as a support group around the life issue you studied, or as a group to study another topic in the LIFESEARCH series.

TIPS FOR LIVELY DISCUSSIONS

TIP 4

Recognize when the silence has gone on long enough. Some questions do fall flat. Some questions exhaust themselves. Some silence means that people really have nothing more to say. You'll come to recognize different types of silences with experience.

TIP 1

Don't lecture. You are responsible for leading a discussion, not for conveying information.

TIP 5

If Plan A doesn't work to stimulate lively discussion, move on to Plan B. Each chapter in this LIFESEARCH book contains more discussion starters and group interaction ideas than you can use in an hour and a half. If something doesn't work, move on and try something else.

TIP 2

Ask open-ended questions. Ask: How would you describe the color of the sky? Don't ask: Is the sky blue?

TIP 3

Allow silence. Sometimes, some people need to think about something before they say anything. The WRITTEN REFLECTIONS encourage this kind of thought.

TIP 6

Let the group lead you in leading discussion. Let the group set the agenda. If you lead the group in the direction you want to go, you might discover that no one is following you. You are leading to serve the group, not to serve yourself.

TIP 7

Ask follow-up questions. If someone makes a statement or offers a response, ask: Why do you say that? Better yet, ask a different group member: What do you think of so-and-so's statement?

TIP 8

Do your own homework. Read the assigned chapter. Plan out possible directions for the group session to go based on the leader's helps in the text. Plan options in case your first plan doesn't work out. Know the chapter's material.

TIP 9

Know your group. Think about the peculiar interests and needs of the specific individuals within your group. Let your knowledge of the group shape the direction in which you lead the discussion.

TIP 10

Don't try to accomplish everything. Each chapter in this LifeSearch book offers more leader's helps in the form of DISCUSSION POINTS, GROUP INTERACTIONS, and other items than you can use in one session. So don't try to use them all! People become frustrated with group discussions that try to cover too much ground.

TIP 11

Don't let any one person dominate the discussion—including yourself. (See "Dealing with Group Problems," page 58.")

TIP 12

Encourage, but don't force, persons who hold back from participation. (See "Dealing with Group Problems," page 58.)

TAKING YOUR GROUP'S TEMPERATURE

How do you tell if your LIFESEARCH group is healthy? If it were one human being, you could take its temperature with a thermometer and discover whether body temperature seemed to be within a normal range. Taking the temperature of a group is more complex and less precise. But you can try some things to get a sense of how healthily your group is progressing.

✓ **Find out whether the group is measuring up to what the members expected of it.** During the CHECKING IN portion of the first session, you are asked to record what members say as they share why they came to this LIFESEARCH group. At a later time you can bring out that sheet and ask how well the LIFESEARCH experience measures up to satisfying why people came in the first place.

✓ **Ask how members perceive the group dynamics.** Say: On a scale from one as the lowest to ten as the highest, where would you rate the overall participation by members of this group? On the same scale where would you rate this LIFESEARCH group as meeting your needs? On the same scale where would you rate the "togetherness" of this LIFESEARCH group?

You can make up other appropriate questions to help you get a sense of the temperature of the group.

✓ **Ask group members to fill out an evaluation sheet on the LIFESEARCH experience.** Keep the evaluation form simple.

One of the simplest forms leaves plenty of blank space for responding to three requests: (1) Name the three things you would want to do more of. (2) Name the three things you would want to do less of. (3) Name the three things you would keep about the same.

✓ **Debrief a LIFESEARCH session with one of the other participants.** Arrange ahead of time for a group member to stay a few minutes after a meeting or to meet with you the next day. Ask for direct feedback about what seemed to work or not work, who seems to be participating well, who seems to be dealing with something particularly troubling, and so forth.

✓ **Give group members permission to say when they sense something is not working.** As the group leader, you do not hold responsibility for the life of the group. The group's life belongs to *all* the members of the group. Encourage group members to take responsibility for what takes place within the group session.

✓ **Expect and accept that, at times, discussion starters will fall flat, group interaction will seem stilted, group members will be grumpy**. All groups have bad days. Moreover all groups go through their own life cycles. Although six sessions may not be enough time for your LIFESEARCH group to gel completely, you may find that after two or three sessions, one session will come when nothing seems to go right. That is normal. In fact, studies show that only those groups that first show a little conflict

56

ever begin to move into deeper levels of relationship.

✔ **Sit back and observe.** In the middle of a DISCUSSION POINT or GROUP INTER-ACTION, sit back and try to look at the group as a whole. Does it look healthy to you? Is one person dominating? Does someone else seem to be withdrawn? How would you describe what you observe going on within the group at that time?

✔ **Take the temperature of the group—really!** No, not with a thermometer. But try asking the group to take its own temperature. Would it be normal? below normal? feverish? What adjective would you use to describe the group's temperature?

✔ **Keep a temperature record.** At least keep some notes from session to session on how you think the health of the group looks to you. Then after later sessions, you can look back on your notes from earlier sessions and see how your group has changed.

LIFESEARCH Group Temperature Record

Chapter 1
_____
_____
_____

Chapter 4
_____
_____
_____

Chapter 2
_____
_____
_____

Chapter 5
_____
_____
_____

Chapter 3
_____
_____
_____

Chapter 6
_____
_____
_____

DEALING WITH GROUP PROBLEMS

What do you do if your group just does not seem to be working out?

First, figure out what is going on. The ideas in "Taking Your Group's Temperature" (pages 56-57) will help you to do this. If you make the effort to observe and listen to your group, you should be able to anticipate and head off many potential problems.

Second, remember that the average LIFE-SEARCH group will only be together for six weeks—the average time needed to study one LIFESEARCH book. Most new groups will not have the chance to gel much in such a short period of time. Don't expect the kind of group development and nurture you might look for in a group that has lived and shared together for years.

Third, keep in mind that even though you are a leader, the main responsibility for how the group develops belongs to the group itself. You do the best you can to create a hospitable setting for your group's interactions. You do your homework to keep the discussion and interactions flowing. But ultimately, every member of the group individually and corporately bear responsibility for whatever happens within the life of the group.

However, if these specific problems do show up, try these suggestions:

✔ One Member Dominates the Group
• Help the group to identify this problem for itself by asking group members to state on a scale from one as the lowest to ten as the highest where they would rank overall participation within the group.

• Ask each member to respond briefly to a DISCUSSION POINT in a round robin fashion. It may be helpful to ask the member who dominates to respond toward the end of the round robin.

• Practice gate-keeping by saying, "We've heard from Joe; now what does someone else think?"

• If the problem becomes particularly troublesome, speak gently outside of a group session with the member who dominates.

✔ One Member Is Reluctant to Participate
• Ask each member to respond briefly to a DISCUSSION POINT in a round robin fashion.

• Practice gate-keeping for reluctant participants by saying, "Sam, what would you say about this?"

• Increase participation by dividing the larger group into smaller groups of two or three persons.

✔ The Group Chases Rabbits Instead of Staying With the Topic
• Judge whether the rabbit is really a legitimate or significant concern for the group to be discussing. By straying from your agenda, is the group setting an agenda more valid for their needs?

• Restate the original topic or question.

• Ask why the group seems to want to avoid a particular topic or question.

• If one individual keeps causing the group to stray inappropriately from the topic, speak with him or her outside of a session.

✔ Someone Drops Out of the Group

• A person might drop out of the group because his or her needs are not being met within the group. You will never know this unless you ask that person directly.

• Contact a person immediately following the first absence. Otherwise they are unlikely to return.

✔ The Group or Some of Its Members Remain on a Superficial Level of Discussion

• In a six-session study, you cannot necessarily expect enough trust to develop for a group to move deeper than a superficial level.

• Never press an individual member of a LIFESEARCH group to disclose anything more than they are comfortable doing so in the group.

• Encourage an atmosphere of confidentiality within the group. Whatever is said within the group, stays within the group.

✔ Someone Shares a Big, Dangerous, or Bizarre Problem

• LIFESEARCH groups are not therapy groups. You should not take on the responsibility of "fixing" someone else's problem.

• Encourage a member who shares a major problem to seek professional help.

• If necessary, remind the group about the need for confidentiality.

• If someone shares something that endangers either someone else or himself/herself, contact your pastor or a professional caregiver (psychologist, social worker, physician, attorney) for advice.

IF YOU'RE NOT LEADING THE GROUP

Be sure to read this article if you are *not* the person with specific responsibility for leading your LIFESEARCH group.

If you want to get the most out of your LIFESEARCH group and this LIFESEARCH book, try the following suggestions.

✓ **Make a commitment to attend all the group sessions and participate fully.** An important part of the LIFESEARCH experience takes place within your group. If you miss a session, you miss out on the group life. Also, your group will miss what you would have added.

✓ **Read the assigned chapter in your LIFESEARCH book ahead of time.** If you are familiar with what the MAIN TEXT of the LIFESEARCH book says, you will be able to participate more fully in discussions and group interactions.

✓ **Try the activities suggested in BEFORE NEXT TIME.** Contributions you make to the group discussion based upon your experiences will enrich the whole group. Moreover, LIFESEARCH will only make a real difference in your life if you try out new skills and behaviors outside of the group sessions.

✓ **Keep confidences shared within the group.** Whatever anyone says within the group needs to stay within the group. Help make your group a safe place for persons to share their deeper thoughts, feelings, and needs.

✓ **Don't be a "problem" participant.** Certain behaviors will tend to cause difficulties within the life of any group. Read the article on "Dealing with Group Problems," on pages 58-59. Do any of these problem situations describe you? Take responsibility for your own group behavior, and change your behavior as necessary for the sake of the health of the whole group.

✓ **Take your turn as a group leader, if necessary.** Some LIFESEARCH groups will rotate group leadership among their members. If this is so for your LIFESEARCH group, accept your turn gladly. Read the other leadership articles in the back of this LIFESEARCH book. Relax, do your best, and have fun leading your group.

✓ **Realize that all group members exercise leadership within a group.** The health of your group's life belongs to all the group members, not just to the leader alone. What can you do to help your group become healthier and more helpful to its members? Be a "gatekeeper" for persons you notice are not talking much. Share a thought or a feeling if the discussion is slow to start. Back off from sharing your perspective if you sense you are dominating the discussion.

✔ **Take responsibility for yourself.** Share concerns, reflections, and opinions related to the topic at hand as appropriate. But keep in mind that the group does not exist to "fix" your problems. Neither can you "fix" anyone else's problems, though from time to time it may be appropriate to share insights on what someone else is facing based upon your own experience and wisdom. Instead of saying, "What you need to do is . . ." try saying, "When I have faced a similar situation, I have found it helpful to . . ."

✔ **Own your own statements.** Instead of saying, "Everyone knows such and so is true," try saying "I believe such and so is true, because . . . ." Or instead of saying "That will never work," try saying, "I find it hard to see how that will work. Can anyone help me see how it might work?" Instead of saying, "That's dumb!" try saying, "I have a hard time accepting that statement because . . . ."

OUR LifeSearch GROUP

Name	Address	Phone Number

FEEDBACK MAIL-IN SHEET

✂ CUT HERE

Please tell us what you liked and disliked about LIFESEARCH:

4. The two things I like best about this LIFESEARCH experience were

5. The two things I liked least about this LIFESEARCH experience were

6. The two things I would have done differently if I had designed this LIFESEARCH book are

7. Topics for which you should develop new LIFESEARCH books are

8. I want to be sure to say the following about LIFESEARCH.

9. I led _____ sessions of this LIFESEARCH book.

FOLD HERE

Thank you for taking the time to fill out and return this feedback questionnaire.

Please check the LIFESEARCH book you are evaluating.
- ☐ Spiritual Gifts
- ☐ Health and Wholeness
- ☐ Juggling Demands
- ☐ Stress
- ☐ Parenting
- ☐ The Environment

Please tell us about your group:

1. Our group had an average attendance of _____ .

2. Our group was made up of
_____ young adults (19 through 25 years of age).
_____ adults mostly between 25 and 45 years of age.
_____ adults mostly between 45 and 60 years of age.
_____ adults 60 and over.
_____ a mixture of ages.

3. Our group (answer as many as apply)
_____ came together for the sole purpose of studying this LIFESEARCH book.
_____ has decided to study another LIFESEARCH book.
_____ is an ongoing Sunday school class.
_____ met at a time other than Sunday morning.
_____ had only one leader for this LIFESEARCH study.

Name_____

Address_____

_____

Telephone_____

Editor, LIFESEARCH series
Church School Publications
P. O. Box 801
Nashville, Tennessee 37202